HELP!

MY ROBOTS ARE LOST IN THE CITY!

I had **14 ROBOTS**, now I have none...

I left the door open, now they've **ALL GONE**!

Forgive me for such a **silly blunder**...

where could they be, **i wonder?**

SPEEDY

is fast just like his name.
Hide and seek is his
favourite game!

HAPPY
BIRTHDAY
PARTY!

MARV

is red like a racing car.
Where could he be,
he can't have gone far!

MR CHIP

loves to watch TV.
I hope he's OK, where could he be?

He's got claws just like a crab.
Can you spot

BORG

in the lab?

P

ARIEL

has a shell, shiny and pink.
Let's find her, what do you
think?

TINKER

has a body made of steel.
He moves around on a single wheel!

Photographers
AMILY PHOTO

Helping people makes him happy.
Can you find

SCRAPPY?

I know he must be around.
So is

RUSTY

anywhere to be found?

DELIVER
express
01

MINI MAX

is a cute little bot.
He's got a face the colour of snot!

ABOVE AND BEYOND

She's very rare. Can you find

DOTTY

anywhere?

SPARKY

likes to smile all day.
I can't find him anywhere,
I hope he's OK.

e
f
a b c
1
2 3

Here's

HECTOR

He's a little shy.
He's blue, just like the sky!

GARDEN
SEEDS
SEEDS

NORBIT

is funny and silly.
I think he's gone
somewhere chilly!

There's only

BOLT

left to find.
Please find him,
if you'd be so kind.

FASHION SHOP
RESTAURANT
FRENCH FOOD

THANK YOU!

The **robots** are found...
and they're coming home
all safe and sound!

A Bonus Search

SPEEDY'S FRIENDS

The **THREE** below are hiding in the book.
Don't believe me? Go take a look!

THE END!

Images and vectors by;

freepix, alekksall, art.shcherbyna, agnessz_arts, anggar3ind, Alliesinteractive, Anindyanfitri, Ajipebriana, Alliesinteractive, Balasoui, Bakar015, Bimbimkha, brgfx, cornecoba, creativepack, creativetoons, d3images, ddraw, dooder, drawnhy97, elsystudio, Emily_b, flaticon, freshgraphix, frimufilms, Garrykillian, gordoba, graphicrepublic, iconicbestiary, ibrandify, Jannoon028, johndory, Kamimiart, katemangostar, kat_branch, kbibibi, Kjpargeter, Kraphix, layerace, lesyaskripak, lexamer, lyolya_profitrolya, Macrovector, Makyzz, milano83, Miguel_ruiz, nenilkime, natalka_dmitrova, natkacheva, omegapics, pch vector, Pickapic, pikisuperstar, rawpixel, Rayzong, renata.s, rezzaalam, rocketpixel, RosaPuchalt, Rwdd_studios, sketchepedia, stephanie2212, SilviaNatalia, Terdpongvector, titusurya, vectorpocket, Vectortwins, Vector4free, vectorportal, vectorpouch, vecteezy, VVstudio, Visnezh, zirconicusso

Printed in Great Britain
by Amazon

46130838R00022